PROVERBS
& SAYINGS

Padraic O'Farrell

MERCIER PRESS
IRISH PUBLISHER – IRISH STORY

MERCIER PRESS
Cork
www.mercierpress.ie

Taken from *Irish Proverbs and Sayings: Gems of Irish Wisdom*
(Mercier Press, 1980)

© Estate of Padraic O'Farrell, 2017

ISBN: 978 1 78117 492 0

A CIP record for this title is available from the British Library

d bound in the EU.

CONTENTS

FOREWORD

Keep your nose in the copy, the pen in your hand and before you know it you'll have a book written.

It was with great enthusiasm that I set about collecting proverbs and sayings for this book. The subject fascinated me. My book *How The Irish Speak English* had absorbed a number of snatches of dialogue which could have been classified as gems of wisdom, but there was a rich harvest still to be gleaned from the Irish countryside, from the lips of great men and from the bright, unspoilt fount of folklore, legend and proverb that still springs whenever Irish people, however long removed from a rural environment, congregate.

I wish to acknowledge the co-operation

of the Head of the Department of Folklore in allowing me to avail of the fine facilities of his department and to peruse and quote from manuscripts and published material. To him and his courteous staff I offer my sincere thanks. I also thank Mrs Fionnula Williams for allowing me to study her thesis, 'Index of the Proverbs of County Monaghan'. This was of immense help in tracing wise sayings, not alone of County Monaghan, but of many other areas too.

Thanks too to my own family, Laurence Gavin, Geraldine Hyland and Patricia Clinton for their assistance.

Padraic O'Farrell, 1980

ADVICE

It's no use giving good advice unless you have the wisdom to go with it.

Ní hé lá na gaoithe lá na scolb.
(A windy day is not the day for thatching.)

Beware of the horse's hoof, the bull's horn and the Saxon's smile.

Never trust a fine day in winter, the life of an old man, or the word of an important person unless it's in writing.

It is foolish to scorn advice but more foolish to take all advice.

When everybody else is running, that's the time for you to walk.

If you dig a grave for others you might fall into it yourself.

Good advice often comes from a fool.

Give the liberty of talking to the loser.

Don't throw away the dirty water until you are sure you have clean water.

If you're advised to use a gun make sure there's not another in your back.

If you have to give advice to lovers, find out what they want first and advise them to do that.

Woe to the man who does not heed the advice of a good wife.

AGE

A hair on the head is worth two on the brush.

No matter what our calling, age will call us all.

The old dog for the hard road and leave the pup on the path.

Strength decreases with age but wisdom grows.

A young woman gets a man's glances, an old woman his heart.

When we are old all our pleasures are behind us but when we are young all our troubles are before us.

The older the fiddle, the sweeter the tune.

It's no harm having plenty of old men in your life as long as there is not plenty of life in the old men.

AMBITION

Keep away from the fellow that was reared in his bare feet, for they will be hardened from walking on people.

Whoever watches for a living man's boots will get sore feet from going barefoot.

On the Irish ladder of success there's always someone on the rung above using your head to steady himself.

The ambitious man is seldom at peace.

Possession never satisfies the ambitious man.

ANGER

A red-hot *gríosach* (ember) is easily rekindled.

The wrath of God has nothing on the wrath of an Irishman outbid for land, a horse or a woman.

Let your anger set with the sun and not rise again with it.

A gentle answer quells anger.

ANIMALS

A man with no wit has little on a pig.

Better an ass that carries you than a fine horse that throws you.

There's no point in keeping a dog if you are going to do your own barking.

You can lead the horse to the well but you can't make him drink.

The horse that wins doesn't lose the reins.

The best colt needs the most breaking in.

Many's the shaggy colt turned out a fine horse.

As the old cock crows the young cock learns.

The quiet pig eats the cabbage.

A nod is as good as a wink to a blind horse.

ATTITUDES

The best way to get an Irishman to refuse to do something is by ordering it.

Pressure of business weakens kindness.

Bigots and begrudgers will never bid the past farewell.

You might as well be hung for a sheep as for a lamb.

Hating a man doesn't hurt him half as much as ignoring him.

Good manners are often better than good looks.

It's the heaviest rain that makes the greenest grass.

The more the storm tries to whip off your happen (clothes) the more you should grip your gallaces (braces).

Initiative is praiseworthy when it succeeds, stupid when it fails.

Titles distinguish the mediocre, embarrass the superior and are disgraced by the inferior.

George Bernard Shaw

Morality is simply the attitude we adopt towards people whom we personally dislike.

Oscar Wilde

BEAUTY

A pot was never boiled by beauty.

It's the gem that cannot be owned which is the most beautiful.

If a mother has no beauty in her face, she has it in her heart.

Elegance and beauty are the same thing when there's a man after them.

Always make sure she looks beautiful before breakfast as well as after dinner.

BEHAVIOUR

He's a dirty bird who won't keep his own nest clean.

Burning the candle at both ends will soon leave you without a light.

If you get the name of being an early riser you can sleep till dinner time.

It is easier to fall than to rise.

If you want to know me, come and live with me.

Keep a blind eye when you're in another man's corner.

Man is either a worker, a boaster or a pleasure-seeker.

The Irish forgive their great men when they are safely buried.

An Irish youth proves his manhood by getting stuck in a pint, in a woman and in a fish – in that order.

The more you step on the dunghill, the more dirt you'll get in.

BITTERNESS

A cranky woman, an infant or a grievance should never be nursed.

The begrudger is as important a part of Irish life as the muck he throws.

Many's the honest man was betrayed by a bitter stepmother.

It's the stones from their father's sloes that children choke upon.

More bitterness is caused by not making wills than by not making up.

A neighbour is comforting in failure and bitter in success.

Sneering does not become either the human face or the human soul.

BLESSINGS

It's a blessing to be in the Lord's hand as long as he doesn't close his fist.

Beware the blessing of a man crossed in love or at an auction.

Here's to a wet night and a dry morning.

3/23

Don't bless with the tip of your tongue if there's bile at the butt.

May we always have a clean shirt, a clean conscience and a bob in the pocket.

May you be across Heaven's threshold before the old boy knows you're dead.

That the tap may be open when it rusts.

Here's to absent friends and here's twice to absent enemies.

May the doctor's shadow never cross your right hand.

BORROWING

Borrowing borrows sorrowing.

Never sleep with a strange woman or borrow from a neighbouring one.

Better an old hat than a borrowed one.

Borrow from a landlord, beg from a tenant.

Never borrow for what you don't need.

Never think you need what you have to borrow for.

BRAVERY

He who faces disaster bravely can face his maker.

If you're the only one that knows you're afraid, you're brave.

It is often braver to live than to die.

The brave and the cowardly last the same length on the battlefield.

CHARACTER

You can take a man out of the bog but you cannot take the bog out of the man.

The mohair suit doesn't hide the bog-dirt under the fingernails.

Better a man of character than a man of means.

Even if you lose everything take care of your good name, for if you lose that you are worthless.

You can't judge a man's respectability by the size of his prayer book.

When you get lime on your *brógs* (boots) it is hard to shake it off.

What is in the dog comes out in the pup.

Don't measure a farmer by his acres but by his heart.

CHARITY

Constant begging meets constant refusal.

A charitable man has never gone to Hell.

The smaller the cottage, the wider the door.

Dispensing charity is the only advantage in amassing a fortune.

Give charity when you can. When you can't it will be too late to acquire the blessing of giving.

CLEVERNESS

An té nach bfhuil láidir ní foláir dó a bheith glic.
(The person that's not strong must be cute.)

Better to be clever than strong.

In spite of the fox's cunning, many a woman wears its skin.

That fellow would cover a rock with hay and sell it as a haycock.

He's as cute as a church mouse and goes to the altar to learn, not to pray.

A clever crook dresses well.

COMMERCE

A verbal agreement is not worth the paper it's written on.

When the cards are on the table it's no time for playing the joker.

Hold on to the bone and the dog will follow you.

Better to have old debts than old grudges.

Short accounts make long friends.

Forgetting a debt doesn't pay it.

If you buy what you don't want you might have to sell what you need.

Better to go to bed supperless than to rise in debt.

The lazy tailor has a long stitch.

COMPANY

The man that's full of *nohawns* (sayings) will never have an empty hearth.

If you lie down with dogs you'll rise with fleas.

Cherish company that does not carry woe on its sleeve.

The loneliest man is the man who is lonely in a crowd.

When you want to be alone be sure there's no chink in the shutters.

I want his company as much as a *méagram* (headache) wants noise.

Talk to yourself rather than to bad companions.

Make a dog your companion and you'll learn to bite.

Don't keep company with your betters. You won't like them and they won't like you.

Even the scabby sheep likes to have a comrade.

Constant company wears out its welcome.

COMPETENCE

The ebb-tide will not wait for the slow man.

Every cripple finds his own way of dancing.

Well begun is half done.

The incompetent talk, the competent walk.

Even if you are on the right track, you'll get run over if you just stay there.

The man that knows what to overlook is the best trained in his job.

CONTENTMENT

Firelight will not let you read fine stories but it's warm and you won't see the dust on the floor.

Enough is as good as plenty.

What you haven't got you won't miss.

If you have one pair of good soles it's better than two pairs of good uppers.

If you want to be out of your house more often, then you should be at home more often.

Be happy with what you have and you'll have plenty to be happy about.

The far-off hills are greener but the one you climb to work is not as steep.

If you never come up in this world you'll never go down in the next.

A share is often enough.

DEATH

There is no use in crying when the funeral is gone.

Ireland's only improving business is under-taking.

Many a day we shall rest in the clay.

Death looks the old in the face and lurks behind youth.

May you never die until you see your own funeral.

Death is the poor man's physician.

Funeral offerings will not buy salvation.

The keening is best if the corpse left money.

There's many a dry eye at a moneylender's funeral.

Never shave a corpse alone for fear your hand would slip and you'd be accused of murder.

There's no respect for the living if they ail during a long winter, nor for the dead if their funeral is during harvesting.

Dead men tell no tales but there's many a thing learned in a wake-house.

Better the trouble that follows death than the trouble that follows shame.

There are more lies told in a wake-room than in a courtroom.

Better an ounce of flour for the living than a ton of sympathy for the dead.

You cannot tell whether the old sheep's or the young lamb's skin will hang from the rafters first.

DRINK

It's the first drop that destroys you; there's no harm at all in the last.

A man takes a drink; the drink takes a drink; the drink takes the man.

You've never seen a flag day for a needy publican.

Before you call for one for the road be sure you know the road.

Practice makes perfect, there's many do think, but a man's not too perfect when he's practised at drink.

Drink is the curse of the land. It makes you fight with your neighbour. It makes you shoot at your landlord – and it makes you miss him.

He'd step over ten naked women to get at a pint.

If Holy Water was porter he'd be at Mass every morning.

The longer the journey the shorter the time for knocking back the jar.

A narrow neck keeps the bottle from being emptied in one swig.

A man in need of a drink thinks of wiser schemes than the great generals of our time.

The truth comes out when the spirit goes in.

Morning is the time to pity the sober. The way they're feeling then is the best they're going to feel all day.

Thirst begets greater thirst.

EDUCATION

A knowledgeable man frowns more often than a *duine le Dia* (person of God, a simple person).

What everybody knows is hardly worth knowing.

No use having the book without the learning.

Youths and fools are hardest taught.

The pen is mightier than the sword – but only in the hand of a just man.

A knowledge of evil is better than evil without knowledge.

Learning is a light burden.

A backward child won't learn anything by starting at the end of the book.

If you keep giving your children comics they'll never read *War and Peace.*

Don't start to educate a nation's children until its adults are learned.

A scholar's ink lasts longer than a martyr's blood.

The schoolhouse bell sounds bitter in youth and sweet in age.

Activity is the only road to knowledge.

George Bernard Shaw

Education is an admirable thing, but it is well to remember from time to time that nothing that is worth knowing can be taught.

Oscar Wilde

ENEMIES

When an enemy offers you a favour, stay close to your own.

Never meet an enemy in a fight or in court.

Better the coldness of a friend than the sweetness of an enemy.

A nation's greatest enemy is the small minds of its small people.

Bid good day to your enemy but listen for his footsteps behind you when you pass.

Put an Irishman on a spit and you'll soon have two Irishmen turning him.

Better fifty enemies outside the house than one inside it.

EXPERIENCE

An experienced rider doesn't change his horse in midstream.

Never give a haikey (inexperienced youth) his will or a pup his fill.

An old broom knows the dirty corners best.

The wearer knows best where the boot pinches.

You cannot know what's around the next bend of the road until you start walking.

Be a man's trade bad or good, only by experience will he master it.

Experience is a hard school but a fool will learn in no other way.

If you know every weed in a boreen you'll not fall into its potholes.

An old dog sleeps near the fire but he'll not burn himself.

If a man fools me once, shame on him. If he fools me twice, shame on me.

A burnt child dreads the fire.

The lesson learned by a tragedy is a lesson never forgotten.

It's no use opening the gate of opportunity if we have not learned to walk through it.

Experience is the name everyone gives to their mistakes.

Oscar Wilde

FAMILY

You can't weigh worries but many a mother has a heavy heart.

Bricks and mortar make a house but the laughter of children makes a home.

Praise and scold in equal measure, if your family you treasure.

A wise boy makes his father happy but a foolish one is a mother's sorrow.

Children won't make you laugh at all times but neither will they make you cry.

Níl aon tinteán mar do thinteán féin.
(There's no hearth like your own.)

What the child sees is what it does.

The herd gathers together when the wolf calls.

No man ever wore a scarf as warm as his daughter's arm around his neck.

Your son is your son today but you have your daughter forever.

He is short of news that speaks ill of his mother.

Poets write about mothers, undertakers about fathers.

A family of Irish birth will argue and fight, but let a shout come from without and see them all unite.

A family is never as close as when it's in mourning.

The family that has no skeleton in a cupboard has buried it instead.

No son is as good as his father in his sister's eyes. No father is as good as his son in his mother's eyes.

A woman is never a mother till she has a son; a man is never a father till he has a daughter.

Children begin by loving their parents. After a time they judge them. Rarely, if ever, do they forgive them.

Oscar Wilde

FATE

If you're born to be hanged, you'll never be drowned.

Many a ship is lost near the harbour.

The apple will fall on the head that's under it.

No matter how long the day, night must fall.

The fox that leaves the covert when the hounds are in the glen seals his own fate.

A pitcher that's often taken to the well will get broken in the end.

What brings death to one brings life to another.

If a man is his own ruin let him not blame fate.

An oak is often split by a wedge from its branch.

FIGHTING

Better to come in at the end of a feast than at the beginning of a fight.

Quarrelling dogs get dirty coats.

The quarrelsome man is lucky. Everybody has to put up with him except himself.

Keep in with the bad man for the good man won't harm you.

If wars were fought with words, Ireland would be ruling the world.

Attackers can never be attacked.

If we fought temptation the way we fight each other we'd be a nation of saints again.

The pup's mother teaches it to fight.

A minute's parleying is better than a week's fighting.

An Irishman is seldom at peace unless he is fighting.

We fought every nation's battles and the only ones we did not win were our own.

Nothing is ever done in this world until men are prepared to kill one another if it is not done.

George Bernard Shaw

As long as war is regarded as wicked it will always have its fascination. When it is looked upon as vulgar, it will cease to be popular.

Oscar Wilde

The first blow is half the battle.

Oliver Goldsmith

This contest is one of endurance and it is not they that can inflict the most, but they who can suffer the most who will conquer.

Terence MacSwiney

FLATTERY

If you're going to tell a girl you're leaving her, tell her she's beautiful first.

What really flatters a man is that you think him worth flattering.

George Bernard Shaw

FOOD

A fast cook causes a faster pain.

Kissing is as sweet as good cooking, but it doesn't satisfy as long.

It takes a lot of hard work to turn a bitter damson into a sweet jelly.

Food is gold in the morning, silver in the afternoon, but lead at night.

Butter's dear bought when it's licked off a briar.

An army may march on its stomach but a husband always makes love on it.

Feed him the finest brown bread and he'll stay, but feed him on clokes and forever he'll stray.

You must crack the nuts before you can eat the kernel.

God give you better meat than a galloping hare.

The first drop of soup is the hottest but the most wholesome lies below.

Eaten bread is soon forgotten – except when it's baked by a complaining wife.

The dog that buries his bones is either well fed or well advised.

FOOLISHNESS

A fool and his money are easily parted.

There's a fool born every minute and every one of them lives.

It doesn't take much to make a fool laugh.

Only a fool burns his coal without warming himself.

There's no fool like an old fool.

Never take the thatch off your house to buy slates for a neighbour's.

Never call a Kerryman a fool till you're sure he's not a rogue.

It's as foolish to let a fool kiss you as it is to let a kiss fool you.

FRIENDSHIP

A boy's best friend is his mother and there's no spancel stronger than her apron-string.

There's no war as bitter as a war between friends.

There never was an old shoe without an old stocking to fit into it.

Friendship is love without its wars.

The best way to make friends is to meet often; the best way to keep them is to meet seldom.

A friend's eye is the best mirror.

In times of trouble you know your friends.

A husband should use his wife's shoulder to cry on.

GOD

You worship God in your way and I'll worship Him in His.

God gave us two ears and one mouth and we should use them in the same proportion.

God is merciful but the Devil help us if He ever gets vexed.

God's help is closer than the door.

Only the grace of God is between the saddle and the ground.

If you haven't been taught by God you'll not be taught by man.

God is ill-disposed to a lying tongue.

Only the Lord can save a racehorse from being a jackass.

GOODNESS

If better were within, better would emerge.

Good begets good.

The bag of apples is never full of rotten ones.

There's more good in a countryman's little finger than in the white hands of all the city's clerks.

Goodness is woman's greatest beauty.

GREED

Every man is born clean, clever and greedy. Most of them stay greedy.

You can't take more out of a bag than what's in it.

The greedy pike gets caught the quickest.

Gluttons have least taste.

The greedy man stores all but friendship.

Greed in a family is worse than need.

The greedy dog licks the honey on the briar.

HEALTH

A woman doesn't have to go out to get the best medicine for her man.

A swelled head won't hurt as much as a swelled toe, but it's a far greater malady.

A good laugh and a long sleep are the best cures in the doctor's book.

Life's physician prescribes humour.

Eat an apple going to bed,
Make the doctor beg his bread.

Young blood should never be cold.

Obesity makes corpses hard to coffin and hard to carry.

A healthy man is a king.

Begin with a cough and end with a coffin.

Work never killed a man but play is often the best medicine.

No time for your health today; no health for your time tomorrow.

HEAVEN

If you have a roving eye it's no use having the other one fixed on Heaven.

The best way to make sure you see a person in Heaven is to see little of him on earth.

Heaven's *leac na teine* (stone before the hearth) is reserved for the poor.

The best matches are made in Heaven.

The shoulders under the coffin have often jostled the corpse out of Heaven.

HELL

The paving stones on the road to Hell have
the weeds of lust binding them.

Needs must when the Devil rides from Hell.

The elbow on the bar counter points the way
to Hell.

A drinking husband, a flighty wife,
Make Hell on earth of family's life.

Walk the road to Heaven but carry the map
of Hell.

If you meet the Devil leave room for him to pass.

HOPE

There's no flood that doesn't subside.

There are finer fish in the sea than have ever been caught.

A man in love keeps moping.
A woman in love keeps hoping.

'I hope to' is a weak man's way of refusing.

He who has never hoped can never despair.

There's nothing that trouble hates facing as much as a smile.

There's nothing so bad that it could not be worse.

The bluebells are found in the deepest forest.

HUMOUR

If he has a purple countenance and no humour, leave him to the priests.

A sense of humour is not a burden to carry, yet it makes heavy loads lighter.

A man that can't laugh at himself should be given a mirror.

A woman in the home is a treasure; a woman with humour in the home is a blessing.

Humour, to a man, is like a feather pillow. It is filled with what is easy to get but gives great comfort.

HYPOCRISY

Before you shake the right hand of an enemy make sure he's not a *ciotóg* (left-handed person).

Even a tin knocker will shine on a dirty door.

She who smiles at the door scowls in the kitchen.

She who kisses in public often kicks in private.

A cat purrs before it scrapes.

The man that hugs the altar-rails does not always hug his own wife.

IDLENESS

A busy mother makes an idle daughter.

The Devil finds work for idle hands.

You'll never plough a field by turning it over in your mind.

It's a worthless hen that won't provide for herself.

It's a poor family that can't afford one gentleman. It's a rich family that can't afford one idler.

INFORMERS

An informer can't mend his ways. He'll inform until he's in his grave and even then you should be careful with the first shovel full.

More Irish graves were opened by the mouth than by the shovel.

A whisper in an enemy's ear is louder than a shout from a mountain.

INTEGRITY

It's harder to become honest than it is to become rich.

What is got badly goes badly.

You don't have to live with the man you cheat but you have to live with your conscience.

When an Irishman talks of 'principle' he is a danger to everybody.

Frank O'Connor

A little sincerity is a dangerous thing and a great deal of it is absolutely fatal.

Oscar Wilde

If one tells the truth, one is sure, sooner or later, to be found out.

Oscar Wilde

JUSTICE

If Ireland had acquired as much justice as abuse she would be the greatest nation on earth.

Those who make the laws are often their greatest breakers.

To every cow its calf and to every book its copy.

King Diarmaid (c. 560)

Do not do unto others as you would they should do unto you. Their tastes may not be the same.

George Bernard Shaw

LOVE

A lad's best friend is his mother until he's the best friend of a lassie.

Love is like stirabout, it must be made fresh every day.

Love at first sight often happens in the twilight.

If you love her in *giobals* (rags) your love will last.

There's little love until there is a fight.

If she has a mind of her own there won't be many with a mind for her.

Never cross a woman who has been crossed in love.

Love cools quickly.

A flicker that warms is better than a blaze that burns.

Every thrush thinks her mate sings the sweetest.

Love is intoxicating. It pleases at first and then sends its victim reeling.

Love is like sun to a flower – it invigorates the strong but wilts the weak.

If a man is in love he is no judge of beauty but when love wears off he'll tell a woman about her warts.

There is no love sincerer than the love of food.

George Bernard Shaw

LUCK

Better to be born lucky than rich.

Lady Luck didn't flirt with many Irishmen.

The lucky shot won't kill the Devil.

The daughter that's minding the parents is always in the byre when good luck is in the haggard.

Good luck is better than early rising.

It's an ill wind that blows nobody good.

Never put the *mí-ádh* (bad luck) on your benefactor.

There is luck in sharing and pluck in refusing.

MAN

Men are like bagpipes: no sound comes from them till they're full.

A man is a man when his woman is a woman.

A sea wind changes less often than the mind of a weak man.

Greatness in a man knows modesty.

A man's fame lasts longer than his life.

A man works hard for success and then squanders his time talking about it.

No man can prosper without his woman's leave.

Man can climb the highest summits, but he cannot dwell there long.

George Bernard Shaw

A man who is not afraid of the sea will soon be drowned.

John Millington Synge

The reasonable man adapts himself to the world; the unreasonable one persists in trying to adapt the world to himself.

George Bernard Shaw

MARRIAGE

Marry a scalder (unfledged bird) and she'll want to rove the world.

A dumb wife and a blind husband might make their marriage work.

Marry a mountainy woman and you marry the mountain.

What harm if your man strays? He mightn't wish to be making a hack out of his best hunter.

A shameful wife makes her husband stick out in a crowd.

Marriage changes a man and makes the woman that changed him whine about his not being the same man she married at all.

Young people bother their parents about getting married. When they're married they are bothered themselves.

A bad wife takes advice from everybody except her husband.

The only thing in the world that's better than a good wife is no wife.

No use buying a bandage for your wife's head when you've broken it.

There'll be white blackbirds before an unwilling woman ties the knot.

Never advise an Irishman to marry or go to war – he's too hot-tempered for either.

He's walking her out that long 'tis an ease to the shoe-leather for them to be married.

Marriages may be made in Heaven but the raw materials come from hell.

Marriage is popular because it combines the maximum of temptation with the maximum of opportunity.

George Bernard Shaw

Whatever joys await the blest above, no bliss below like happy wedded love.

William Allingham

Women begin by resisting a man's advances and end by blocking his retreat.

Oscar Wilde

MEANNESS

He'd skin a flea for a ha'penny and sell the hide.

A mean act is long felt.

Small minds utter small words.

The mean deed turns on the man that did it.

She's so mean she'd get the cat to chew her meat in order to save her delph (false teeth).

There's little difference between a closed hand and a fist.

If she's mean at the table she will be mean in the bed.

They're so mean they'd give you one measle at a time.

He'd steal the cross off an ass's back.

MISFORTUNE

'Tis a misfortune for a man to cut a *bonnsog* (twig) to beat himself.

Beidh lá eile ag an baorach.
(The underdog will have his day.)

You never miss the water till the well runs dry.

An Irishman sees his profit after his misfortune.

When misfortune is greatest, relief is nearest.

The latest misfortune is the greatest misfortune.

Misfortune sends no warning.

MISTAKES

God only made one mistake – he allowed mistakes to happen.

When fools make mistakes they blame Providence.

Do not mistake a *meigeall* (goat's beard) for a fine stallion's tail.

Correct your own mistakes from those made by others.

The wise man doesn't know his master's mistakes.

MONEY

The best way to keep loyalty in a man's heart is to keep money in his purse.

The hardest man to tire is the money-lender.

Money borrowed is soon sorrowed.

Money is a good servant but a bad master.

Money taken, freedom forsaken.

A wage is the amount of money a man lives on; a salary is the amount he spends.

A poor tinker would like to have a rich man's problems.

The man who asks what good is money has already paid for his plot.

The man who pays the piper calls the tune.

Money is the root of all evil, but avarice is the compost.

As the money bag swells, the heart contracts.

Wealth is an uncertain prop.

When I was young I thought that money was the most important thing in life; now that I am old I know that it is.

Oscar Wilde

NATURE

The brightest sunshine is after the rain.

It only takes one bad potato to destroy what's on the *gais* (stalk).

The tallest flowers hide the strongest nettles.

A wild goose never reared a tame gosling.

It takes every blade of grass to make the meadow green.

The cow doesn't always take after its breed.

What's in the marrow comes out in the bone.

There's no tree but has enough rotten twigs to burn it.

NEED

Words are as much needed as stones in Clare.

Necessity is a virtue.

If you are without sheep you have to be your own dog.

Need is the beginning of greed.

The man with a cow doesn't need a scythe.

He's so needy he couldn't give up eating his nails for Lent.

PATIENCE

Patience is a virtue,
Have it if you can;
It's seldom in a woman
And never in a man.

The apple won't fall till it's ripe.

Patience will heal the most itching scar.

If you push the carrier to the well he might
fall in.

Patience cures many an old ill.

Patience and forbearance made a bishop of His Reverence.

If you rush the woman the spuds will be hard.

Stepping stones will get you across the stream of life.

The cow won't have her calf till she's ready.

The greatest need for patience is when waiting your turn for the settle.

The only thing more blessed than patience is a silent woman.

POLITICS

A turkey never voted for an early Christmas.

A patriotic politician will always lay down your life for his country.

A statesman is a dead politician.

The Dáil is the only place in Ireland that is powered by hot air and where noise travels faster than light.

A politician is a man who can find a problem in every solution.

An ambassador is a politician who can do less harm away from home.

The last move in politics is reaching for the gun.

The successful political leader can divide the national cake so that everybody thinks he's getting a slice.

There's nothing like a few shots to change the fanatic into a non-partisan.

In matters of grave importance, style, not sincerity, is the vital thing.

Oscar Wilde

He knows nothing and he thinks he knows everything. That points clearly to a political career.

George Bernard Shaw

[A Political] Party is the madness of many for the gain of a few.

Jonathan Swift

PRIDE

Stoop as you walk the path of life and you'll not be struck by the branch of pride.

He fancies himself so much that his mother is trying to remember were the shepherds looking on when he was born.

Pride may have a fall and if it's family pride it brings a few with it.

Pride never stops growing until it's ready to challenge God.

The gentry's pride prevents their seeing the beauty of humility.

PROPERTY

A good lease with a bad landlord is better than the best landlord in the country and no lease. Best of all would be the country without either landlord or lease.

Half a loaf is better than no bread.

Better to own a little than to want a lot.

Your friends are as big as what you own.
If that is small you're all alone.

If you don't own a mount don't hunt with the
gentry.

A poor man never lost his property.

Where there's a will there's a fray.

A dog owns nothing, yet is seldom dissatisfied.

Many an Irish property was increased by the lace of a daughter's petticoat.

Land and horses are properties dearest to an Irish heart.

Play with the woman that has looks, talk marriage with the woman that has property.

ROGUERY

She'd cheat the devil in the dark and take two
farthing candles for a ha'penny.

He'd cod you out of the sight of your eye and
tomorrow come back to steal off with the stye.

You cannot plough a straight furrow in a
crooked field.

If he gives you a rope he might stand at your
back while it's hanging you.

SCARCITY

One shower in a drought is about as good as a grasshopper's spit.

Fruit is sweetest when it's scarcest.

A crippled *ciaróg* (beetle) could look over the heap of potato-skins on the table.

You won't find many *pusthagauns* (conceited people) in the workhouse.

There's little need to keep a cat when all the mice in the house will die of malnutrition.

SENSE

If commonsense rules from your head to your feet you'll not wear a dunce's cap or walk a wrong road.

Beware the woman that has more between her stays than between her ears.

On an unknown path it is better to be slow.

The man with sense doesn't talk before breakfast.

Don't put a giddy man at the tiller.

Even a rock of sense should move when there's danger.

The man who rows the boat does not rock it.

The gossips were all busy in the corner when God was giving out sense.

It's no use sending a chicken to bring home a fox.

A blind man should not be sent to buy paint.

It's no use carrying an umbrella if your shoes are leaking.

If you don't fry over an open fire you'll never get burned.

SORROW

There's nothing as sorrowful as a mother without her children.

Happiness always has a little sorrow mixed through it.

A lone woman has a sorrowful row to hoe.

Be sorry for the jealous man.

We learn in suffering what we teach in song.

SPENDING

Easy come, easy go,
but having to spend what's hard got is a blow.

The son spends fast what his father hoarded
long.

Spent money causes no rows.

If he doesn't spend when he's single, he won't
give when he's not.

Don't give your purse to a lender.
And don't give your heart to a spender.

SPORT

You can't decide a tug-of-war contest by cutting the rope with a knife.

If I bet on the tide it wouldn't come in.

If that goalkeeper put his head in his hands it would slip through.

Eternal hope means eternal hunger for the gambler's family.

STRENGTH

Muscles won't bend a strong man's will.

The strong obey when the stronger order.

The strong man may when he wishes; the weak man may when he can.

It's not the strongest that live the longest.

Where strength shows, strength grows.

The man with the strongest character is attacked most often.

TACT

Don't crow till you're out of the wood.

A diplomat must always think twice before he says nothing.

Never talk about a rope in the house of a hanged man.

If you wish a favour from a man, sit beside him. If you wish a rebuke sit in his seat.

Never talk about the blow that's not yet struck.

Tact is clever humility.

If you say everything you want to say, you'll hear something you don't want to hear.

TALK

A kind word never got a man into trouble.

Speak neither well nor ill of yourself.

A slip of the tongue is no fault of the mind.

English is all right for huckstering but the Irish language should always be used in lovemaking.

Leave the bad news where you found it.

There's grit in the butt of a rival's praise.

Kind words never split any man's lip.

You can easily win an argument if you start off by being right.

Don't believe half of what you see or a quarter of what you hear.

Every man is wise till he speaks.

If words were nails we'd have built a great nation.

Silence is the fence around the haggard where wisdom is stacked.

Those who talk the loudest about a man while he is alive whisper the lowest in the mortuary.

Medicine goes in through the mouth but there's no medicine will save a fellow that uses his mouth too much.

Argument is the worst sort of conversation.

Jonathan Swift

Questions are never indiscreet. Answers sometimes are.

Oscar Wilde

You need not praise the Irish language – simply speak it.

Patrick Pearse

THANKS

Say 'Please' to the judge for you won't be able to say 'Thanks' when the hangman's job is done.

Never look a gift horse in the mouth.

If you beg on a foolscap, don't thank on a postcard.

THEATRE

A theatre critic doesn't serve his time to his trade – but he should serve time for his work.

An actor who says he doesn't read the reviews is neither a coward nor an egotist – he's a liar.

There are two types of theatre critic. One thinks he's God Almighty, the other is sure of it.

If there's coughing during the first scene they won't be using their hands for clapping.

The world is a stage but the play is badly cast.

Oscar Wilde

TIME

Time and tide wait for no man.

Time is longest to the waiting man.

Time brings the sweetest memories.

Time is the best *seanachaidh* (storyteller).

Don't be too busy to kill time.

When God made time he made plenty of it.

Waste my money but don't waste my time.

The busy man is the man who makes time to help.

VALUE

The man that knows the price of everything knows the value of nothing.

True value comes in dull wrappings.

An empty house gives better value than an owing tenant.

A shack is valuable to a poor man.

Give good value and the good will come back.

WEARINESS

It's as long as a wet Sunday and as dreary as a wet Easter.

If the knitter is weary, the baby will have no new bonnet.

WISDOM

A man begins cutting his wisdom teeth the first time he bites off more than he can chew.

There's more wisdom spat into the *griosach* (embers) than you'd pick up in a year's book-learning.

A questioning man is halfway to being wise.

There's no wise man without some fault.

An apple can't grow on a crab tree and a wise man won't bear a fool.

Wisdom makes a weak man strong, a poor man king, a good generation of a bad one and a foolish man reasonable.

WOMAN

She mightn't be much good to boil a pot of spuds but she'd look lovely carrying them to the table.

Women would drive you mad but the asylum would be a cold place without them.

There's nothing more vicious than a woman's temper except, maybe, a woman's tongue.

The foolish woman knows the foolish man's faults.

I wouldn't like to be hanging by the neck since she was thirty.

It is not the most beautiful woman who has the most sense.

Everything dear is every woman's fancy.

Never be in a court or a castle without a woman to make your excuse.

The weak grip of a woman holds tighter than a vice.

An excuse is as near to a woman as her apron.

A woman's beauty never boiled a pot but her ugliness never filled either it or her.

It takes a woman to outwit the Devil.

Wherever there are women there is talking and wherever there are geese there's cackling.

Where comes a cow, there follows a woman,
Where comes a woman, there follows trouble.

Let her rant and rave as long as the sun is high and as long as she's loving, close and tender when the sun sets.

A woman who looks at the window is edgy,
A woman who gazes into the fire is worried.

WORK

Work as if there was fire in your skin and you'll never be without a fire in your hearth.

Work for one thing and you'll gain another.

The ass that brays the most eats the least.

The mason that lays fifty bricks will die no sooner than the one that lays twenty.

Praise if you wish progress.

The best blows to strike for Ireland are the blow of the sledge on the anvil, of the axe on the block, of the flail on the stone.

If you'd prefer to be doing something else, you're working.

Hard work and good care take the head off bad luck.

You won't be able to tell how much money a man is earning by looking at his clothes but you will by looking at his wife's.

Do your job well and eat your fruits with relish.

Work hard, work long and have nothing to worry about – but in doing so don't become the boss or you'll have everything to worry about.

Work is the refuge of people who have nothing better to do.

Oscar Wilde